Should any Christian ever be baptized?

Ray Downen &
Marion Owens

ISBN 978-1-60658-024-0
*
Printed by:
KOINONIA ASSOCIATES
7809 Timber Glow Trail
Knoxville, TN 37938
web: PublishwithKA.com
*

"You were BAPTIZED INTO union with Christ"

(Galatians 3:27) The apostle Paul.

INDEX

SINNERS are invited to repent and be baptized into Christ, and to *<u>then</u>* receive both (1) remission of and cleansing from sins, and (2) the "gift of the Holy Spirit!" Many scripture passages speak to the fact that the Holy Spirit does sanctify, and that His work is essential for our salvation no less than that of Jesus who died for us. But some seem unaware that the work of the Spirit is not done in those who are not yet in Christ!– Ray Downen.

Should any Christian ever be baptized?

by Ray Downen

Foreword: Why should anyone be baptized? Jesus commands baptism. Some Christian teachers are now being heard to teach that it's Christians who need to be baptized – to signify to others that they have been saved by Jesus. If these teachers are correct, then shouldn't we be baptized again and again and again as the years pass, perhaps at least once per year? Marion and Ray say no Christian should ever be baptized. What is baptism for? I'm suggesting that as part of the new birth of water and spirit, baptism as commanded by Jesus is to create Christians. Peter explains why sinners should repent and be baptized.

Here Marion & I explain what the Bible does teach about how sinners become Christians. Some do agree with Peter (1 Peter 3:21) that baptism does save. Some will disagree, claiming that the apostle Paul teaches that the baptism which saves is performed by the Holy Spirit. And many insist salvation depends only upon faith. *Jesus commissioned that **we who love Him** are to carry the gospel message everywhere we go in this world and then that **WE humans are to baptize into Christ those repentant non-Christian hearers who now believe the message about Jesus, the risen Lord.***

I quote here a teacher who affirms that conversion into Christ precedes the baptism commanded by Jesus. Reflections 362 (9/2/2008). This does not agree with what the Bible teaches. A phrase in Paul's letter to the Corinthian church, so far as I know, is in the only verse which might justify what some teach about a baptism by the Holy Spirit. The verse, 1 Corinthians 12:13 can easily be misunderstood. The phrase in question concerns baptism "in one spirit." The verse was apparently written by one who obviously believed a baptism brings sinners into fellowship with Jesus and His church. **Seth Wilson points out that this exact same phrase, "in one spirit" is used**

by Paul *and correctly translated* in Philippians 1:27:

> *Only let your manner of life be worthy of the gospel of Christ, so that . . . I may hear of you that* ***you are standing firm in one spirit****, with one mind striving side by side for the faith of the gospel, and not frightened in anything by your opponents.* –

The subject to be discussed is "baptism *in one spirit*."

Look carefully at I Corinthians 12:13

Were the baptisms spoken of in 1 Corinthians 12:13 performed "in one spirit" as the apostle here also wrote, or "by the one Spirit" or "by one Spirit" or "in one Spirit," as many translators say? In the English Standard Version the verses read,

> *"For just as the body is one and has many members, and all the members of the body, though many, are one body, so it is with Christ. For* ***in one Spirit*** *we were all baptized into one body—Jews or Greeks, slaves or free—and all were made to drink of one Spirit."* (ESV 1 Corinthians 12:12,13).

Compare: the American Standard Version of 1901, then Holman's Christian Standard Bible and the New International Version, and last, the King James Version:

> "For **in one Spirit** were we all *baptized into one body,* whether Jews or Greeks, whether bond or free; and were all made to drink of one Spirit" – 1 Corinthians 12:13 (ASV).
>
> "For we were all *baptized* ***by one Spirit*** *into one body*—whether Jews or Greeks, whether slaves or free—and we were all made to drink of one Spirit"– 1 Corinthians 12:13 (HCSB).
>
> "For **by one Spirit** are we all *baptized into one body,* whether we be Jews or Gentiles, whether we be bond or free; and have been all made to drink into one Spirit" 1 Corinthians 12:13 (KJV).

Be reminded that Jesus commissions in Matthew 28 that the gospel should be preached and taught everywhere and ***those who believe are to be baptized by the ones who carried His message to them.*** I suggest that we best understand the Lord's teaching by seeing how the apostles, led by His Spirit, understood what they were to do and what we therefore also are to do.

Did you notice in every translation, "all were baptized INTO *one body*? Is not Paul here saying that baptism marks a **change** in relationship, that in their baptism sinners are changed, buried with Christ and raised ***into new life*** (Romans 6:1-14)? Resurrected, as was Jesus. The man of sin is buried. A Christian is born. New birth is INTO Christ and His church.

Every translation of 1 Corinthians 12:13 speaks of being baptized, with the baptism *followed* by action involving the Spirit. Peter agrees. Why do some now disagree with Paul and Peter?

You will note later that one now says Paul was not writing about baptism at all in this passage. Or **is** that what he thinks? I understand him to now claim that Paul teaches that the Holy Spirit violently *plunges* the former sinner into Christ's church. But rather than to create any action by the Spirit, Paul is writing here about *our need to remain united in Christ Jesus!*

Apostles baptized sinners INTO Christ

The verse quoted above says baptism is INTO the body we call the church. We hear many now saying that baptism does NOT bring sinners *into Jesus and His church.* Does 1 Corinthians 12:13 not claim it does? Some teach that the action which brings sinners into the church is not the baptism commanded by Jesus, but is an action performed by the Holy Spirit. But note that a baptism BY the Spirit is spoken of only in some translations of this one verse. **Never anywhere else in apostolic writings is such a thing even hinted at.**

The *only* passage in apostolic writing which speaks of a baptism by the Spirit is what I see as a wrong translation of the verse quoted above, 1 Corinthians 12:13. The latest translations seek to more correctly bring into English what the apostle wrote. So they have him writing about a baptism IN (rather than BY) the Spirit. *But why would anyone think Paul might have contradicted himself by speaking of a second baptism to be performed either by* ***or in*** *the Spirit? Paul knew* **there was only**

one baptism commanded by Jesus and *it was for* His *followers to perform.* *We also should know this.* In this study we suggest what reference to baptism the apostle obviously makes in 1 Corinthians 12:13.

The article and letters and rebuttals which follow refer to publications by AL MAXEY in which he seems to take the position that an action which saves is performed by the Holy Spirit the instant that a sinner realizes that Jesus is the risen Lord and deserves to be obeyed. Repenting and being baptized in water may follow, he says, but does not cause or affect this supposed "baptism by the Holy Spirit." It is a separate action. And lately he is not recognizing the Spirit's action of which he speaks as being baptism, preferring to call the baptism a "plunging."

You will see that he is teaching that water baptism is an "act of faith" that a Christian should take some time when that's convenient. Does baptism save? Or is it just for show? These are different ways of looking at the baptism commanded by Jesus. This teaching about conversion is found in an Al Maxey Reflections article #353 (6/26/2008) and see Reflections #212 (10/3/2005) on the new birth of water and spirit. And Al Maxey's Reflections article, #528 (4/9/2012) reflects his understanding that conversion occurs without the sinner receiving baptism in water.

His most recent book, in January 2012, expands on what Marion and Ray see as, at best, wrong understanding. I hear Al Maxey saying he is convinced that conversion is based on faith alone as something done TO rather than BY the convert. I see Al as very wrong indeed in this understanding of entering the Way of Christ, for is he not ignoring the examples of conversion any reader of Acts should study? In this book I quote his testimony that he was converted to a Calvinistic view of conversion as a student of the Greek language. He now is trying to convert others to that view while he aims to continue as a part of an undenominational fellowship of Christians-only. Our reformation pioneers rejected Calvinistic teaching on conversion because they saw it was not rightly dividing the word of truth.

What do Calvinists believe about the new birth of water and spirit? Does Calvinist belief differ from what some of "us" are now teaching? As you later read quotations and citations from Al Maxey, compare them to this linked statement of Baptist (Calvinistic) beliefs, from which I quote only Article 5. http://www.bpnews.net/BPnews.asp?ID=37939.

> Article Five: The Regeneration of the Sinner. We affirm that any person who responds to the Gospel with repentance and faith is born again through the power of the Holy Spirit. He is a new creation in Christ and enters, at the moment he believes, into eternal life. We deny that any person is regenerated prior to or apart from hearing and responding to the Gospel. Luke 15:24; John 3:3; 7:37-39; 10:10; 16:7-14; Acts 2:37-39; Romans 6:4-11; 10:14; 1 Corinthians 15:22; 2 Corinthians 5:17; Galatians 2:20; 6:15; Colossians 2:13; 1 Peter 3:18.

Article Nine deals with eternal security and should be considered by anyone wanting to understand Baptist doctrine. As you read Al's writings, I hope you will compare his teaching with the above statement of Baptist beliefs.

***

Begotten for New Life

The goal of the reformation of which I am a part is that all Christians should love one another and together work to win the world to Jesus **while teaching Bible truth.** Marion and Al are also part of this reformation movement. How does new life begin? Doesn't it start with a seed? Farmers or gardeners plant a seed. When the seed germinates and is watered, a plant comes forth. In animals the female body produces seeds which die unless fertilized.

In Luke 8 and in Matthew 13 we read of gospel seed which is "planted" within human hearts. That seed in many cases produces spiritual life which leads to eternal life as each person obeys the gospel. Through the shared story of Jesus and His love, the "seed" of the gospel is planted and can grow. The process is described by James.

James writes, *"Submit to God and **accept the word that He plants in your hearts, which is able to save you**"* (James 1:21). Paul repeats this theme by mentioning to Galatian Christians that God had given to them His Spirit *because they had heard and believed (and, of course, then obeyed) the gospel* (Galatians 3:5). The apostle reports that as a result of his having preached the gospel in Corinth, converts to that gospel could consider him as their spiritual father (1 Corinthians 4:15 and 3:6). The gospel of Christ as it was heard, believed, and obeyed in repentance had begotten them for eternal life. They still had to complete their new birth in water baptism. Jesus and His apostles speak of the new life which is possible through our death to sin and resurrection "*into* new life" as we are baptized.

BORN AGAIN INTO New Life

Paul explains, *"It is through FAITH that all of you are God's sons in union with Christ Jesus. **You were BAPTIZED INTO union with Christ**"* (Galatians 3:26,27). Human birth requires a begetting to precede and effect (cause) the actual birth. Are there not equally two steps in the new birth of water and spirit? Peter explains that the begetting for spiritual rebirth is through sinners hearing and obeying "the **word** of Christ." Please ponder:

> (1 Peter 1:22-25 – ESV) *Having purified your souls by your obedience to the truth* for a sincere brotherly love, love one another earnestly from a pure heart, since *you have been born again, not of perishable seed but of imperishable,* ***through the*** *living and abiding* ***word*** *of God; . . .* ***this word is*** **the good news that was preached to you.**"
> And 1 Peter 1:3-5 (ASV) "3 ... **Jesus Christ**, who according to his great mercy **begat us** again ..."

Sinners who learn about Jesus and His offer of salvation are urged to then turn away from sin and to follow Jesus as Lord, says the apostle as reported in Acts 2:38. Our spiritual new birth comes through our obedience to that gospel call. We turn to Jesus and accept baptism into Him *because that's what the Word teaches is how to enter the Way.* In John 3:1-6 John reports that *Jesus told Nicodemus that those who wanted to enter His kingdom must do so by way of a new birth of both water and spirit.* Jesus did not speak of a new birth of water and "the Spirit." The original language says simply "water and spirit." This was a new birth of water and spirit – a **spiritual rebirth** which climaxed in baptism into Christ. The *new birth of water and spirit* is contrasted with the **fleshly birth experienced by every human**.

> Now there was a man of the Pharisees named Nicodemus, a ruler of the Jews. This man came to Jesus by night and said to him, *"Rabbi, we know that you are a teacher come from God, for no one can do these signs that you do unless God is with him."* Jesus answered him, *"Truly, truly, I say to you, unless one is born again he cannot see the kingdom of God."* Nicodemus said to him, *"How can a man be born when he is old? Can he enter a second time into his mother's womb and be born?"* Jesus answered, *"Truly, truly, I say to you, unless one is born of water and the Spirit (spirit), he cannot enter the kingdom of God. That which is born of the flesh is flesh, and that which is born of the Spirit (spirit) is spirit"* John 3:1-6 (ESV. Translators capitalize the word "spirit." Why?).

This rebirth was more fully explained by Peter when seeking sinners asked him (Acts 2:37), "What must/can/shall we do?" They realized they were lost in sin. They sought redemption. Peter explained clearly what any sinner must do in order to be saved and brought into the body of Christ. If we believe that Jesus is Lord, then in order to enter His Way we must turn away from sin, turning to Jesus as our Lord, and we must be immersed in water in response to His command that this is to be done. Peter did not call this saving process a new birth, but since he's answering the question which pertains to entering the Kingdom of Christ, we may know that he's simply restating what Jesus had privately told Nicodemus several months earlier about entering the "kingdom of God."

We believe Christ's kingdom on earth are the people we call God's church in every land. 3,000 that first day when the gospel was preached were added to the Lord's body. The indwelling Spirit is promised to all who meekly receive (they believe and consent to obey) the implanted word which is Christ's gospel (James 1:18,21) and are then baptized in the name of Jesus. In faith that the gospel story is true, believers in Jesus who repent and are baptized are spiritually reborn as babes in Christ. We then receive remission of sins and the gift of the indwelling Spirit of God (Acts 2:38).

In the new birth we are reborn of water and spirit and *then* receive God's Spirit within. Chapters 6-8 of Romans, and 1 Corinthians 12:13 help us understand how we are reborn *and are promised that God then will live within us.* It's for unity with Jesus and His people that we are spiritually reborn and brought into His church! The apostle Paul in 1 Corinthians 12:13 urges that all who are in Christ should realize the unity into which we were baptized. Our baptisms were identical. No one gets baptized better than anyone else did. And these identical baptisms brought us, and continue to bring new repentant believers, into the one body of Christ. We should recognize and respect our unity in Him.

The baptism of which Paul speaks in Ephesians 4:5 and in Galatians 3:27 and in 1 Corinthians 12:13 and in Romans 6 are each the same baptism which Jesus commanded that men should perform whenever a new believer repented of sin and sought salvation in Christ. *Baptism in water is part of the new birth which brings new Christians into Christ and into His body.* If our loyalty is to Jesus Christ, through new birth of water and spirit we become part of the "one body" which is Christ's church. Jesus prayed that we would realize and actualize our unity in Him (John 17).

But perhaps in 1 Corinthians 12:13 Paul was saying the baptism was performed by God's Spirit (some translators think it's IN one Spirit, baptized by Jesus Himself) rather than in a spirit of repentant humility. Some want to think so. In Philippians 1:27, this same phrase *"in/by one spirit"* is used to modify *"standing firmly for truth."* It's *us who claim to belong to Jesus* who are to stand firm. It's US who are to stand for truth and it's US who share the unifying baptism into Christ which brought us all into His one body.

Confusion is created by poor translation

Paul surely did not seek to create by his phrase, baptized "in one spirit" a second baptism or some "plunging" which had been performed by the Holy Spirit. **Those who translate his words in this way (BY or IN one Spirit) are creating confusion rather than clarity.** And Al doesn't successfully mask his teaching of a second baptism by claiming that here the word should be read as "plunge" instead of "baptize." Those to whom Paul wrote all knew, and Paul knew also, *they* had been baptized INTO Christ and into His church through an immersion (baptism) in water from which each had been raised into new life.

The same "in one spirit" phrase is used in verse 3, referring to confessing faith in Jesus as the Christ. No one is inspired by God's Spirit to deny that Jesus is God's unique Son and Word. Those who deny Jesus surely are never helped in such a denial by God's Spirit. We who come to believe in Jesus are urged to say so on every occasion. We who love Him and are born again have the presence of His Spirit to help us testify for Him. God acted in creating new life within as we heard the Word of truth, and as we turned away from sin, and as we were baptized into Christ and into His body. That's what Paul has said.

Peter also says it's the immersion in water which follows faith and repentance that brings us into new life in Christ. In the Bible, Galatians 5, 2nd Peter, and Romans 12 tell us more about the effect of inviting God to rule in our hearts. Jesus speaks of us receiving this power by remaining attached to "the vine," which He says is Himself. If we do "abide in the vine" where the power of Jesus is present, Paul says the fruit produced in our lives will be "fruit of the spirit" as contrasted to "fruit of the flesh" which leads some to spiritual death. See the listings in Galatians 5 to contrast bad and good fruit. **Paul is contrasting what others choose over what we who seek godliness and goodness will see resulting from our good choices.** Good spiritual fruit is love, joy, peace, longsuffering (patience), kindness, goodness, faithfulness, meekness, and self-control. Shouldn't these be the fruit we each want in our life?

Peter also urges us to seek and to produce such fruit by us *adding to our faith* goodness, knowledge, self-control, endurance, godliness, brotherly love and love (2nd Peter 1:3-9). Many passages contrast the results of our allowing fleshly appetites to lead us astray or else <u>our spiritual desires</u> to be our guide and helper. None of these passages suggest that God will miraculously bestow any of these characteristics on anyone. How we live is *our choice*. What we seek, we will find. What we go after, we receive. Peter calls for **us** to do the adding to our faith. He doesn't say God will add these things while we sit idle or spend our time praying for Him through His Spirit to do the work of making us over.

Who understands truth?

Do only those possess the Spirit who understand all truth just as you or I do? Not likely. Is knowledge and correct understanding of apostolic teaching a special gift of the Spirit? We can see this is surely not the case. The unity God desires for His church will not be brought about by a miraculous gift of knowledge which enables all Christians to entirely agree on apostolic doctrine. It hasn't been that way. It won't be that way. We should not today expect miraculous wisdom and knowledge to be sent to us in place of our personally reading and studying the Bible. And by our making and keeping good resolutions.

Jude warns that God's message was "once for all delivered." And the writer of Hebrews admonishes us about our need to be attentive to the message of Jesus and His apostles, for there'll not be a new and differing message sent to us by God. James invites us to seek God's help when we want to know truth (James 1:5). Paul prayed for Ephesian Christians, so they could see the revealed truth, that God would give them "a spirit of wisdom and of revelation in the knowledge of Him" (Ephesians 1:17,18). This is similar to his use of "in one spirit" in 1 Corinthians 12:13. And he wrote, "I pray that the eyes of your heart may be enlightened."

John writes, ***"But you have had the Holy Spirit poured out on you by Christ, and so all of you know the truth,"*** (1 John 2:20) and *"As long as His Spirit remains in you, you do not need anyone to teach you, for His Spirit teaches you about everything"* (1 John 2:27). If John meant that every person hosting Christ's Spirit (remember that everyone who is in Christ is gifted with the Holy Spirit as a result of their new birth of water and spirit) would fully and perfectly understand Christian doctrine, how can we account for the dissension over doctrine from the first century even until now? Which of us has His Spirit? Does God's Spirit lead us to differ? Surely not!

Who is led into "all truth"?

Our brother CECIL MAY, JR. in his PREACHER TALK for January, 2012, points out:

> As part of a lengthy conversation with the twelve (apostles), Jesus said, "I still have many things to say to you, but you cannot bear them now. When the Spirit of truth comes, he will guide you into all the truth" (John 16:12,13a). Evangelicals frequently claim that promise for themselves, believing that the Spirit both enlightens their minds to better understand the written word and leads them in their daily lives.
>
> Jesus was certainly addressing his apostles when he said these words, and all evangelicals believe the apostles were endowed with special powers including the gift of authoritative inspiration. Therefore, it makes good contextual and exegetical sense to understand this promise as made exclusively to the apostles.
>
> If the promise is to every believer, it leads to an unfortunate conclusion that the Holy Spirit leads Christians into a

wide variety of questionable, sometimes contradictory positions. Or if, as the Roman Church maintains, the promise applies beyond the twelve to the future church, we face the equally troublesome conclusion of the teaching authorities of the church adding "authoritative" revelation and interpreting Scripture as they wish with impunity.

The Spirit guided the apostles into all truth and the hidden mysteries of the gospel are now revealed to us "through his holy apostles and prophets by the Spirit" (Ephesians 3:5).

We are the losers if we today rely only on human means when we seek knowledge. God hears and answers prayer. We should faithfully, earnestly pray for His guidance and help whenever we face any decision or determination. But it is wrong to pray and then make no effort to meet the need we recognized. And we are never told to pray to the Spirit. Just as lazy Christians are not miraculously made diligent workers, patient, loving, and unselfish (against their will and inclinations), neither are we blessed with knowledge of God's will when we refuse or neglect to read and study and believe His Word.

We learn by reading inspired writings

Seth Wilson says that what the Spirit provides Christians today is a motive and state of heart in which we can make determinations of doctrine. The same laws of language and logic apply to the Bible as to any other written work. God will help us learn. We should not be hesitant to ask for His help. But He doesn't give us a substitute for the Word which was once for all delivered to the saints. God's Spirit *does not give us new and different instructions from God than are in the apostolic writings.* We also should realize that not all who quote scripture prove truth by their quotation. When the devil was tempting Jesus, each temptation was accompanied by a quotation from the Bible. Yet Jesus refuted and refused each temptation. Obviously then, **Bible quotations can be used to mislead.** Seth Wilson notes that sly scholars, or fervent and faithful followers, may twist truth by misunderstanding or misapplying Bible passages. We who hope to recognize truth need to keep our wits about us and "handle aright the word of truth." Should we call on God to do for us what we could have done for ourselves? Through study and prayer, we can understand the Bible. We need to read it for ourselves and consider what has been revealed.

Why does it ever seem possible for us to change a teaching or decision we thought came to us directly from God? We have to realize that possibly an understanding which we now see does not agree with God's revelation came to us from some other source than the One who inspired men to write Bible books. In order to learn truth, Christians should study the Bible as well as to pray for guidance. Apples grow on apple trees. Oranges don't grow there, or bananas. God has arranged that each tree and plant should produce its own fruit rather than some other kind. As a normal result of walking with Jesus in new life, ***every true Christian will produce good spiritual fruit.***

Seth Wilson suggests that by God's provident power, and by my selfless surrender, the spirit of love, joy, peace, etc. will gradually displace my human self-centered spirit with its evil fruit. Drinking from the vine to Whom we are attached will drive out Satan's seductive spirit. The process of maturing in Christ is called "growing" in Him. A healthy, well-fed child grows to the limits set by God. Needed growth just happens. That's God's plan. Babes in Christ also will grow as they feed on "the vine." To become like Christ is to be filled with His Spirit, and this should be the goal of each of us who have turned to Jesus seeking light and life. We want to be like Jesus. The more we know about Him and His life on earth, the more apt we are to be successful in our goal of becoming like Him. We learn of Jesus and His will for us by study of apostolic writings.

Baptism in, and special gifts of, the Spirit

Special gifts of the Spirit are mentioned only a few times in Acts, and then in Paul's letters to the Corinthian Christians. They were unusual. Most Christians had none of these "special" gifts of the Spirit. Yet some in our day want to make special spiritual gifts the center of their preaching and practice. We need to put our emphasis where Jesus wants it. We have no proof He wants emphasis on us rather than on Him.

As for *baptism in the Spirit,* it was sent upon the apostles and only upon them to make *them* special, to empower *them* for the work they were to do. But God wants us to realize that OUR baptisms should unite us all as equal parts of His church. We are not apostles. We have no clergy set apart from others in the body. From among us we select pastor/teachers, and evangelists, and others, for special service. But we have no popes or cardinals or presidents or other dignitaries who hold congregational offices which make them superior to others in the church of the Lord. Every elder is a bishop for in the Bible the titles "elder" and "bishop" refer to the same people.

There is no baptism in or by the Spirit for Christians today. The Spirit is given to every sinner who in faith repents of sin and is immersed into Christ, but this is not a baptism in the Spirit. It is not a baptism by the Spirit. His Spirit is God's gift to all who because of faith in Jesus and repentance from sin are then buried with Jesus in immersion in water from which we are raised into new life. Life in Christ begins as we hear about Him. Buried in water and raised into new life, we who are in Christ were each *baptized into* Him and into His one body.

We are called then to maintain the unity of Christ's body. Even when we see matters differently, as we surely will, we are to LOVE one another. It's by our shared love that others will recognize that we are in Christ. If we were begotten by the Word of God, if we were reborn of water and the spirit, if we now seek to be filled with and possessed by Christ, we are sure to be lovers rather than fighters, uniting rather than dividing Christ's body.

Next I offer for your thought a totally different idea about conversion than what the Bible teaches. It's from one who has adopted salvation by faith-only thought and still claims to be teaching Bible truth. Al Maxey in his Reflections article #515 for 1/3/2012 concerning Acts 2:38 comments on conversions. His study can be read on the internet. I quote it as written. I comment first, however, about his speaking of us who believe Bible truth as being "baptismal remissionists."

We who teach Bible truth are not "baptismal remissionists." Nor do we understand Acts 2:38 as "evangelicals" or "sacramentalists." Is the writer first quoted by Al creating a straw man so it can be knocked down? What we know the apostle clearly says is not at all what we see is suggested in Al's introductory statement as our view. What WE find in what IS said is not what Al by quoting others claims that we teach. *The clear instruction by the apostle was that believing* ***sinners*** *needed to both repent AND be baptized for the remission of sins and to receive the gift of the Spirit.*

WE are not claiming that baptism is a sacrament. We don't cite Acts 2:38 or any other passage to prove anything at all about baptism **alone. What we aim to do is to just teach what the apostles taught and are reported to have practiced.** We have not, as is alleged, depended on the meaning of only a single word or any single verse for our understanding. Nor have we tried to impose on the conversions reported in Acts any "conversion theory" other than the one revealed by Luke.

Acts 2:38 speaks to needed human response to the gospel. God's part in conversion is done. It was done at Calvary and in the giving of the great commission. Man's part is based on hearing and believing and obeying revealed truths. So OUR part in conversion is indeed based on what we learn and what we do. We see no need to try to tell God what to do. We preach/teach the gospel to tell what God has already done. And then we repeat the apostolic call for sinners to save themselves by obeying the gospel.

Did the 3,000 who in Acts 2 were baptized into Christ have access to the passages Al suggests are needed in order to correctly understand what Peter said? **Or do you suppose they just believed Peter knew what they needed to do?** I think they just understood and obeyed simple truth. As we also surely should do! Truth is not changed by later revelation from God which very possibly may expand on the truth but *will never change it.*

Does Al do what he claims we are doing?

The only verse which speaks of a baptism by the Holy Spirit is the way some translators have mishandled 1 Corinthians 12:13. This started with the King James Version or before. *It might seem that Al has built a theology around the wording in English as handed down from the old King James Version rather than from any correct handling of that one verse.* Many passages show that baptism in water is part of the new birth of water and spirit. I refer readers to my study, RAISED INTO NEW LIFE, Part 1, available from amazon.com on the internet. *I agree that we should not build doctrine based on only one verse or by ignoring context.* No one should do so. But isn't Al doing so? He quotes many Baptist scholars to disprove Acts 2:38.

Conversion by Faith-Alone Teaching Examined –

Al Maxey writes about Peter's Words in Acts 2:38

"On the surface, in English, it seems that by what he said as recorded in Acts 2:38 Peter meant that the purpose of baptism was to effect the remission of sins, which explains why baptismal remissionists so readily appeal to this verse" [E. Calvin Beisner, "Does Acts 2:38 Teach Baptismal Remission?," *Christian Research Journal*, vol. 28, no. 2]. Yes, "on the surface, in English, the words of Peter do indeed *seem* to promote such a view, but deeper study and reflection show the matter to be a bit more complex than some would have us believe. In reality, 'Acts 2:38 assuredly confronts the interpreter with weighty problems,'" says Professor Stonehouse, "and the extent and diversity of the theological exegesis of the verse show how right he is" [Dr. F. F. Bruce, *Commentary on the Book of Acts*, p. 75].

Dr. A. T. Robertson, one of Christendom's greatest New Testament Greek scholars, agreed, saying that this verse "is the subject of endless controversy as men look at it from the standpoint of sacramental or of evangelical theology" [*Word Pictures in the New Testament*, e-Sword]. "Peter's answer to the people's anguished cry presents interpreters with a set of complex theological problems that are often looked upon only as grist for differing theological mills" [*The Expositor's Bible Commentary*, vol. 9, p. 283].

Unfortunately, this is absolutely correct. Disciples of Christ have fussed, fought, feuded and fragmented over Acts 2:38 for centuries! Vastly differing theologies have each embraced this passage as the validation of their view, resulting only in greater confusion than clarity. Much of this is a result of a failure to fully perceive both the grammar and structure of the passage as it appears in the Greek text, preferring instead to build a theology around the wording in English as handed down from the old *King James Version*.

Additionally, by lifting a passage from its overall context, one can easily do damage to the original intent of the author, thus *abusing* the verse to further a tradition, rather than *using* it to further Truth. "Rarely is doctrine ever made from a single verse" [Matt Slick, "Baptism and Acts 2:38," *Christian Apologetics & Research Ministry*]. One must examine carefully and prayerfully ALL of what the Bible says with respect to a topic, not just lift a handful of passages out of context to prove a personal or party perception or preference. Sadly, I fear we have done too much of the latter with respect to Acts 2:38.

The reality of God's inspired revelation, and this is perceived *throughout*, is that **we are saved by grace through faith, not by virtue of anything we have done or ever could do; rather, it is a gift of God because of His great love and mercy.** If this is true, and I believe with all my heart that it is, then we must repent of proclaiming a performance-based and knowledge-based salvation! *[Ray comments: So, Al says, "Peter, repent!"]*

Redemption is not to be found in getting religious rituals right; it is found in the redemptive act of our Redeemer! Salvation is a GIFT, and it is received by FAITH. Yes, genuine faith will *show* itself in our daily lives in countless loving manifestations, but none of these evidentiary acts, in and of themselves, constitute the precise point of salvation (as some sacramentalists assert). Thus, passages like Acts 2:38 must be understood in view of the truth that "it is by grace you have been saved, through faith—and this not from yourselves, it is the gift of God" (Ephesians 2:8). {RAY: Peter says, "Repent *and be baptized...*"}

With that foundational truth in mind, how are we to understand what Peter told the people in Jerusalem on that first Pentecost following our Lord's death, burial, resurrection and ascension? Peter's message in his sermon was essentially: Jesus is the Messiah . . . . and you killed Him . . . Repent of this, and embrace Him! Dr. F. F. Bruce correctly points out that in Acts 2:38 "the call to repentance is Peter's basic and primary demand" (*Commentary on the Book of Acts*, p. 75). When we teach *baptism* as the primary demand of this verse we have missed Peter's point. {RAY: Peter says, "Repent ***and*** *be baptized...*" We echo Peter's call.}

Peter's purpose was to *turn the hearts* of his hearers to faith in Jesus as their Redeemer, who, by virtue of His shed blood, would cleanse them of their sins! This basic emphasis is especially seen in Peter's sermon in Solomon's Colonnade where he says nothing about baptism, but instead declares to the people, "Repent, then, and turn to God, so that your sins may be wiped out" (Acts 3:19). "This shows that for Luke at least, and probably also for Peter, while baptism with water was the expected symbol for conversion, it was not an indispensable criterion for salvation" [*The Expositor's Bible Commentary*, vol. 9, p. 284].

Peter's clear emphasis is *repentance*, which "is not a mere feeling; it has not the uncertainty of moods and sentiments. It is not a simple change in the weather of the soul. It is a distinct alteration of the focus of the intelligence; it carries with it a movement of the will; in short, it is a revolution in the very ground of the man's being" [*The Pulpit Commentary*, vol. 18, p. 66]. {RAY: Peter says, "Repent ***and*** *be baptized...*"}

The "Baptismal Remissionists," however, insist that the word "for" in Acts 2:38 proves otherwise! Yes, the people were to *repent*, but forgiveness of sins came at the point of *baptism*, they declare. After all, Peter said to be baptized "FOR the forgiveness of your sins." Thus, sins are forgiven AT baptism! Right?! Again, "on the surface, in English," this wording does seem to promote such a view . . . *until* one begins to look a bit deeper and to ask some vital questions. For example, what do the rest of the New Testament writings have to say about forgiveness of sins and how such forgiveness is acquired? [RAY: Was Peter wrong? Al thinks so!]

Paul makes the case, in Romans 4, that Abraham's transgressions were forgiven and his sins covered *by faith*, and that it was a gift of God's grace *prior* to his circumcision. Was circumcision an outward rite to which this man was required by God to submit? Yes, it was. But, as Paul notes, his forgiveness and justification were *not* due to this outward act, but rather based upon his *faith*.

Paul goes farther here and informs us that this principle is true for us under this new covenant. Forgiveness, justification, salvation are not based on our acts of faith, but upon faith itself. The various acts (of which baptism is one) are merely evidentiary in nature: they *show* faith (James 2). They are *essential* (no one is denying that fact), but they themselves are not *redemptive* (as some claim). Thus, *baptism does not remit sins, but evidences one's faith in and acceptance of the One who does!* [Ray: Is that what Paul taught? No.]

However, we are still faced with that little word "for" in Acts 2:38. Because of that word, some will vehemently assert that everything I have just said is "false teaching," and thus "Al Maxey is a heretic who denies baptism." Nothing could be farther from the truth. Water baptism is an act commanded by our Lord. Thus, we must comply. I have baptized many people during the years of my ministry, and I anticipate baptizing a great many more. I preach and teach the importance of water baptism, and I practice it. What has changed for me, however, is my previous perception that water baptism is *the* specific act *by* which, and *the* precise point in time *at* which one is forgiven, justified, redeemed, saved, etc. I will no longer proclaim baptism as a *sacrament*, but rather as a required manifestation of one's faith. [RAY: Why ever call baptism a sacrament?]

Forgiveness comes to those who turn from sin and in faith turn to the Lord. Such persons then *demonstrate* that inner faith and repentance by a number of visible acts that will occur throughout their lives (one of which is baptism). But, can one justify this view that forgiveness comes to those who by faith have turned to the Lord, or does the word "for" suggest it is *baptism* that brings the blessing? I believe one can make a strong case, from the structure and grammar of the Greek, for the former. And furthermore, if such an understanding of the text is at least a legitimate one textually and exegetically, then that fact would forever remove Acts 2:38 as a proof-text for baptismal remissionists. {RAY: Peter says, "Repent ***and*** *be baptized...*"}

"A Bible verse *proves* a doctrine only if that doctrine is the only interpretation the grammar and word definitions permit. If there are other plausible interpretations, the verse might be used as evidence in a cumulative case for the doctrine, but its evidential value rises or falls in inverse proportion to the plausibility of the other options" [E. Calvin Beisner, "Does Acts 2:38 Teach Baptismal Remission?," *Christian Research Journal*, vol. 28, no. 2]. So, let's take off our sectarian spectacles and seek to view this passage with fresh spiritual sight.

First, we need to realize that the word "for" in Acts 2:38 is *not* the actual word used in the Greek text (more about that word later). Nevertheless, even the English word "for" has quite a wide variety of meaning and usage. In *Webster's New International Dictionary*, for example, there are ***eleven*** definitions of the preposition "for" given, and baptismal remissionists have assumed that only *one* of those definitions can apply in this passage: that it denotes purpose, and signifies "in order to obtain."

Although other legitimate definitions of "for" make equal sense, they are nevertheless discarded. Why? Because they don't support their theology! For example: "for" may also mean motive, thus signifying "because of." Would this definition of "for" in Acts 2:38 make sense? Would it be consistent with New Testament teaching? Of course it would. So, *why* is one chosen dogmatically over the other? I think we all know the answer to that.

Is this other usage of "for" found in the New Testament writings? Yes, it is. In Matt. 3:11, just to give one instance, we find John the Baptist saying, "I baptize you with water ***for*** repentance." Okay, are they baptized "in order to obtain" repentance? That doesn't make sense. But, being baptized "because of" their repentance makes sense (and, by the way, this is the Greek preposition "***eis***" here, just as it is in Acts 2:38). {RAY: Peter says, "Repent ***and*** *be baptized...*"}

When words have a variety of meaning and usage, we must allow the context in which the word appears, as well as the overall teaching of Scripture, to dictate which usage best fits. And where *several* may fit, one dare NOT become dogmatic over his interpretive choice. "The plausibility of these alternative understandings of '*for*' reduces the evidential value of Acts 2:38 for the doctrine of baptismal remission of sins" [E. Calvin Beisner, "Does Acts 2:38 Teach Baptismal Remission?," *Christian Research Journal*, vol. 28, no. 2].

The English word "for," however, is just a translation of the Greek preposition "***eis***," but, like the former, the latter also has a wide variety of meaning and usage, including the two mentioned above. "The illustrations of both usages are numerous in the New Testament and the *Koine* generally" [Dr. A. T. Robertson, *Word Pictures in the New Testament*, e-Sword]. Therefore, there are times when the Greek preposition *eis* (which appears some 1774 times in the NT writings) refers to purpose, and there are times when it refers to motive (and times when it refers to something else entirely). Again, one must allow the context, as well as comparative study of New Testament teaching on the topic in question, to guide one's understanding of the preposition in any given passage. Yes, baptism *for/eis* (purpose) the remission of sin is a valid rendering of the phrase, but is it a valid teaching in light of the doctrine of salvation by grace through faith. I do not believe it is. {RAY: Peter says, "Repent ***and*** *be baptized...*"}

On the other hand, baptism *for/eis* (motive) the remission of sin, which is also a valid understanding of the phrase (and is the view taken by such Greek scholars as A. T. Robertson and J. R. Mantey, just to name a couple), IS consistent with the doctrine of salvation by grace through faith. We are washed clean of our sins by the precious blood of the Lamb, and we reflect the reality of that spiritual washing in the symbolic rite of baptism, which is a testimony and affirmation not only to ourselves, but also to others (much like our partaking of the elements of the Lord's Supper, by which we participate emblematically with the reality itself). Thus, we are baptized *because of* our forgiveness, not in order to *obtain* forgiveness. The latter elevates a sacrament; the former elevates the Savior!!

Baptism in water is "the visible seal of that remission" of our sins [Jamieson, Fausset and Brown, *Commentary Critical and Explanatory on the Whole Bible*, e-Sword]. "Water baptism is the external symbol by which those who believed the gospel, repented of their sins, and acknowledged Jesus as their Lord publicly bore witness to their new life" [*The Expositor's Bible Commentary*, vol. 9, p. 284]. Most Christians recognize that "there is nothing in baptism itself that can wash away sin. That can be done only by the pardoning mercy of God through the atonement of Christ" [Albert Barnes, *Notes on the Bible*, e-Sword]. {RAY: Peter says, "Repent ***and*** *be baptized...*"}

The renowned NT Greek scholar, Dr. A. T. Robertson, in his classic work "*Word Pictures in the New Testament*," declared, "My view is decidedly against the idea that Peter, Paul, or anyone in the New Testament taught baptism as essential to the remission of sins or the means of securing such remission. So I understand Peter to be urging baptism on each of them who had already turned (repented) and for it to be done in the name of Jesus Christ on the basis of the forgiveness of sins which they had already received." Dr. F. F. Bruce agrees, characterizing "baptism as the visible token of repentance" [*Commentary on the Book of Acts*, p. 77]. But, is there anything else in the text of Acts 2:38, either grammatically or structurally, that might perhaps bring additional light, and which might help us in our understanding of Peter's intent? Well, as it so happens, *yes there is*. There is a very significant break in the passage structurally that is not carried over into the English.

"There is a change of number from plural to singular and of person from second to third. This change marks a break in the thought here that the English translation does not preserve" [Dr. A. T. Robertson, *Word Pictures in the New Testament*, e-Sword]. "In Peter's command, the verb *repent* is second-person plural. The verb *be baptized* is third-person singular. In the phrase *for the forgiveness of your sins*, the word *your* is second-person plural again. Imagine the implications of *ignoring* this switch from second-person plural to third-person singular and back again!!" [E. Calvin Beisner, "Does Acts 2:38 Teach Baptismal Remission?," *Christian Research Journal*, vol. 28, no. 2].

This interpretation views *"for/eis"* as signifying *purpose* more than *motive*, but it links it with repentance rather than baptism. In other words, Peter is telling the people that they need to turn away from their present course and turn toward the Lord *in order that* they might receive the forgiveness of their sins. Each one doing so was then to be baptized in the name of Jesus the Christ, the very one they had previously rejected, but were now declaring to be Lord and Savior. That act of faith (baptism) would affirm their faith and bear witness to their new allegiance! It is not the turning itself that forgives sins, but rather the One to whom they turn: Jesus! HE washes clean those who in fullness of faith turn to Him. Such persons then evidence that faith throughout the remainder of their lives (one of the first evidentiary acts being baptism). {RAY: Peter says, "Repent ***and*** *be baptized...*"}

Dr. Beisner wrote, "In short, the most precise English translation of the relevant clauses, arranging them to reflect the switches in person and number of the verbs, would be, 'You (plural) repent for the forgiveness of your (plural) sins, and let each one (singular) of you be baptized (singular).' When I showed this translation to the late Dr. Julius Mantey, one of the foremost Greek grammarians of the twentieth century and the co-author of '*A Manual Grammar of the Greek New Testament*,' he approved and even signed his name next to it in the margin of my Greek New Testament" (*ibid*).

RAY: *Wow! I guess that proves something! And of course it does. It proves that the Calvinistic teacher made a convert to Calvin's doctrine.* And the Calvinist remained in fellowship with Christians who strongly oppose Calvinism and he now seeks to win more converts to Calvin's doctrine.

AL: Let me repeat this principle of biblical hermeneutics: "A Bible verse *proves* a doctrine only if that doctrine is the only interpretation the grammar and word definitions permit. If there are other plausible interpretations, the verse might be used as evidence in a cumulative case for the doctrine, but its evidential value rises or falls in inverse proportion to the plausibil*ity of the other options" [ibid].*

There are clearly a number of ways to understand Acts 2:38, each of which are grammatically legitimate, which fact demands we not become dogmatic with respect to our interpretations. I have my personal convictions as to what Peter sought to convey to the people of Jerusalem that day, and I believe they are textually and contextually and conceptually sound. However, I don't pretend to be infallible in my insights (and I doubt seriously any of you are either), thus I pray we can continue to love and accept one another as brethren to the glory of our God, even when we honestly differ. {RAY: Peter says, "Repent ***and*** *be baptized...*"}

***

Ray Downen's Response

Was Al writing to agree with Acts 2:38 or was he disputing with Acts 2:38? Was Peter wrong? Luke quotes Peter as promising salvation based on sinners repenting and being baptized. The question was "What shall WE DO?" I think Peter spoke the truth. Passages in Acts deal with conversion and include specific examples of actual conversions. Why would any Bible student or teacher suppose he understands better than the apostles did what sinners must do? Did Peter not know the "foundational principle" so dear to proclaimers of salvation by faith alone? Why suppose he gave a wrong or cryptic answer to the question of "What must **we** do?"

I think that Al is saying the apostle Peter was tragically wrong in "proclaiming a performance-based and knowledge-based salvation." That is exactly what Peter did in Acts 2:38 and elsewhere. And the apostles Paul and John agree with Peter! What a shame. I thought the apostles were given the Spirit in baptismal measure so they would be *right* in their teaching! Al IS commenting in this quoted essay about Acts 2:38! What Peter actually said is not agreeable to Baptist thought in any age. It appears as if our brother is saying kindly that the apostle Peter was mistaken or unclear in his speech.

Why does this lengthy article by Al Maxey misunderstand the question being answered? It may be because Peter's answer does not conform to what Al now wants to believe. The 3,000 who heard what Peter said asked what **they** needed to do. Peter told them *what every sinner needs to do* to be saved. They chose to believe and act upon what Peter told them. Then, having obeyed the gospel, the 3,000 that day were added to the Lord's church! That's how it's done. We marvel that some *are so determined to not believe and act in accordance with apostolic teaching!* **The foundation is in Acts 2 being laid by the One Jesus said would know the "rock" (the foundation) upon which the church was built!** The apostles learned from the Lord and taught the truth.

Is it true that salvation by grace through faith **alone** is a rock upon which the church was built? It surely is not! Peter points to the truth. Acts 2:38 is not speaking about God's part in conversion. The apostle is answering the question, "What must WE do?" The straw man was attacked! But **do "we" teach baptism as the primary demand in Acts 2:38? Why would we?** And when did the baptism commanded by Jesus become a "religious ritual"? Is obeying our Lord something to be derided?

What Acts 2:38 calls for is REPENTANCE **AND** BAPTISM, both based on faith in Jesus as Lord. So of course that is what "we" teach and call for. WE are not straw men! If anyone did teach baptism as the primary demand of Acts 2:38, that teacher would be mistaken. But how many times must a truth be stated before it can be believed? Is Acts 2:38 not true since in the next chapter only repentance is mentioned? This seems to be what is implied by Al. Let's consider every conversion reported in Acts! In each case, the convert was immediately baptized. And never was the baptism performed by the Holy Spirit. Was repentance always mentioned? Of course not. We do not therefore imply or believe that *repentance* is not needed!

What Peter in fact said as quoted in Acts 2:38 is that new believers in Jesus as Lord must REPENT **and** be baptized, *after which God would forgive sin and gift them with His Spirit.* He did not, and we do not, claim that baptism alone forgives sin. Yet that is what some are seen to claim we believe and teach. We believe Peter knew what Jesus calls for sinners to do to enter His Kingdom. And we are sure that Jesus would not have His Spirit later contradict what Peter said as recorded in Acts 2:38 or try to explain it away. Nor do we think it is so complicated that it's even hard to understand by those who want to understand it.

And Luke reports that Peter, as his purpose in preaching, *urged his hearers to save themselves!* How? By repenting and being baptized because of faith in Jesus!

Do we all notice that Al, whose announced subject is Acts 2:38, switches to Acts 3, apparently to explain what he thinks Peter SHOULD HAVE said in Acts 2:38? This would have been a good place in Al's lesson for him to have mentioned all the other examples of conversions recorded in Acts. That's what I do in RAISED INTO NEW LIFE. But Al seems instead to want to negate and dispute with what Peter actually said in Acts 2:38! And **does Peter emphasize repentance over baptism** or does he simply link the two equally-needed actions with an "and"?

Teachers of conversion by faith alone must think "for" is a very powerful word! Have you ever heard any other Christian teacher insist that Acts 2:38 can't be understood except with their meaning of "for"? Peter linked repentance **and** baptism with remission of sins. Some want to separate the actions. I never met others than "faith only" believers who insist that the word "for" changes the meaning of Peter's words recorded in Acts 2:38. The new birth of water and spirit brings us INTO Christ. It's not something long drawn out and something we continue to do or that we some time later do as a Christian.

Births sometimes take hours, or frequently are quick. The new birth is normally not long drawn out for weeks and months and years. And surely we know when birth has occurred! They did in the conversions recorded in Acts. Why would we now not know? **Peter calls repenting and being baptized simply submitting to what is required in order to *enter the Kingdom* and have sins remitted.**

I'm confident that Luke in writing about what Peter taught, and what his hearers did, shows they also understood the matter without needing to go to passages not yet written in order to understand Peter's invitation. Other passages need to be understood in the light of what Luke reports that Peter said and how Luke reports that it was understood by those who heard. I hear

Al claiming our understanding of conversion is based on only one verse and on one word IN that verse. This is not in any way a true picture of our understanding of conversion. We believe Peter was speaking truth about what sinners must do in order to be saved by faith in Jesus. But if being baptized truly is like loving and showing compassion, should it be done only once? Repentance is frequent. Living for Jesus is a lifetime occupation. Baptism is a one-time act.

I'm surely glad that Al will not in the future wrongly proclaim that baptism is a sacrament. I'm sorry if he or anyone ever did so. But he is tragically wrong in trying to remove it from the timing Luke reports that it had in the apostolic age, and where Jesus had put it in His great commission.. Baptism was not something to be done *sometime.* It was to be done immediately when a sinner believed in Jesus and turned to Him. Anyone who doubts this should read again the Bible book of Acts. In apostolic times baptizing was done immediately. As soon as belief and repentance came. Luke says in Acts 2 that 3,000 repentant believers were baptized the same day they heard the gospel. And they were that very day added to the Lord's family of faith!

Do we need to repeat the obvious truth that the "for" in Acts 2:38 follows both repenting **and** being baptized? Repenting AND being baptized. Both. And they both must be based on faith in Jesus as the risen Lord in order for them to be "for" the remission of sins through the blood of Christ. Al Maxey is far more concerned than I am about the meaning of the one word "for." Does he imply that readers should believe Peter's words only if they agree with the reader's prejudices? That is not the case. We clearly see that Peter was telling these seekers that BOTH repentance (turning away from sin–**turning to Jesus as Lord**) AND baptism are required as part of the new birth of water and spirit. And THEN the former sinner receives remission of sins AND the gift of the Holy Spirit! We believe so because of Acts 2:38 and several other passages which teach the same truth.

But Al is surely right that "for" has more than one meaning in different uses. In Acts 2:38, the apostle actually said. *"Repent*

AND be baptized for the remission of your sins . . ." He did not say his hearers should repent and then some time later be baptized. Both actions together result in the believing sinner receiving remission of sins and the gift of the Spirit. Sinners repent seeking remission of sins. Sinners repent and are baptized for remission of sins. Baptism is for the purpose of washing away sin, says Paul also (Romans 6:1-11). Both choosing to serve Jesus and being baptized are FOR the remission of sins. That's "in order to receive." Peter here is answering the question, "What shall we DO?"

So Al Maxey accepts "faith-only" doctrine and cites Calvinist scholars while rejecting what is believed and taught in other Christian circles and by common sense. He asks us all to do so as well. I cannot do so. I am a follower of the Christ. Jesus calls for PEOPLE to baptize each new believer. Al and others now say the Spirit will do the baptizing "into Christ!" And he seems to suppose either Luke or Peter and Paul didn't understand what sinners needed to do in order to be saved. Al says the difference within the Greek of Acts 2:38 is "**not** carried over into the English." Of course it is! Repentance is done BY the person. Baptism is done TO the person. The English speaks of this by translating the passage, "REPENT (you do this) AND **BE** BAPTIZED (this is done TO you). Both are for the remission of sins and in order to receive the gift of the Holy Spirit of God. That's what Peter promises will follow new believers repenting and being baptized.

It is not reasonable to suppose that any sincere believer in the inspiration of apostolic writings could fail to see that the church led by the apostles practiced an immersion in water as the baptism Jesus commanded. It therefore is the baptism which brought and brings sinners into the body of Christ which is His church. Not a one of them thought baptism was performed by the Holy Spirit or in/with the Spirit except to the apostles who were empowered by baptism IN the Spirit by Jesus. No apostle teaches that *salvation is by grace through **faith alone*** as Calvin proposes. Repenting and being baptized isn't a sacrament although it is what sinners must do to be saved.

32 *There are* ***no sacraments*** *in the Christian Way.* No apostle ever spoke of any sacrament.

The "scholars" Al quotes are not members of a Church of Christ or a Christian Church which is associated with the Restoration Movement of which I'm a part (Stone-Campbell variety). I am a Christian. Nothing more. Nothing less. I invite every other believer in Jesus to join me in being a "Christian only." We freely associate with and work with all who love Jesus. We form ourselves into independent congregations loyal to Jesus but not to men who might claim to speak for us.

In offering this study, I do not speak for any religious body. I declare what I believe to be truth revealed in the apostolic writings. If aware of what Al Maxey is teaching about conversion to Christ, most of my brethren would join me in opposing what we consider to be false doctrine. But many do not see as I do that Jesus was claiming sinners had to be reborn of water and the human spirit. So some of my brothers in Christ imagine that the Holy Spirit is involved in conversion prior to the time Peter says He is given. Since I believe all scripture is equally inspired and fits together to form truth, I have to believe Peter knew the truth and spoke the truth about when the Spirit is given.

We do well to understand what Al is teaching. Is baptism an act of faith like loving and serving for Jesus? That is what I hear our brother saying. Are we now convinced that baptism is an "act of faith" rather than part of the new birth of water and spirit as Peter teaches? Repentance and being baptized are indeed based on faith in the One who calls for those actions. But the new birth into Christ obviously does not include every act based on faith which should be performed by ones who believe in Jesus. Many scripture passages speak to the fact that the Spirit does sanctify, and that His work is essential for salvation no less than that of Jesus who died for us. But the work of the Spirit is not done in those who are not yet in Christ! Sinners are invited to repent and be baptized into Christ, and **then** receive remission of sins and the gift of the Holy Spirit!

***

After receiving Al's study about Acts 2:38, Marion Owens felt led to comment. I received his comment which follows and then chose to prepare this booklet to explain to anyone who would read it why we felt it desirable to respond to what Al had published to explain away Peter's appeal for sinners to save themselves by obeying the gospel.

BAPTISM AND CONVERSION

by Marion Owens, September, 2011

As a long-time reader of Al Maxey's "Reflections," I am almost always in agreement with him, especially regarding some of the legalistic views which have dominated certain segments of the "Churches of Christ." However, I strongly *disagree* with his repeated contention which reflects the basics of classic "faith-only" doctrine that baptism in water by disciples of Jesus is not part of the conversion process. This essay is being written to support the belief that *water baptism* **is** *an integral part of the conversion process.*

The evidence that baptism is part of the process by which one becomes saved is remarkably abundant and clear. Even if all we had were the words of Jesus, ***"Whoever believes and is baptized will be saved,"*** (Mark 16:16 as it appears in some manuscripts) that should be enough to convince us–but that is only the beginning! [Ray remarks that the baptism in this passage is surely the baptism commanded by Jesus, that is, immersion in water.]

Peter, an apostle who was present when Jesus spoke those words, understood that baptism was part of the process by which one is saved. That's why he told a crowd of cut-to-the-heart believing Jews to **"Repent and be baptized for the forgiveness of your sins"** (Acts 2:38). There was certainly nothing in Peter's words to indicate he thought that their sins were *already* forgiven and that baptism was just some type of symbolic acceptance of that forgiveness!

When was Saul of Tarsus saved?

By all of Al's descriptions of the conversion process, Saul would have been thoroughly saved by the time Ananias got to him (Acts 9:1-19). But Ananias ordered him to **"Get up, be baptized and wash your sins away."** Is it not obvious that Ananias thought when one becomes saved his sins ***are*** **then washed away?** So if Saul was saved and therefore his sins were taken away *before* baptism, why would Ananias have him to wash away the sins *again?* It is clear that Ananias did *not* think that Saul was already saved, but that indeed he still needed to have sins washed away. And Luke does not suggest Ananias was wrong.

Writing to the Galatians, Paul referred to their having been **"baptized into Christ..."** (Galatians 3:27). But if they were saved *before* baptism then they were *already* in Christ prior to the baptism commanded by Jesus. Some have tried to get around the obvious meaning of this passage by trying to place some far-fetched complicated definition on the term "baptized" here. Paul was writing to theologically unsophisticated Christians. The only fair interpretation of his words must be in the context of their understanding of baptism.

It was simple: when as repentant believers they were immersed in water they had moved from a position of being "out of Christ" to a position of being "in Christ"–from being unsaved to being saved–from being burdened with their sins to having their sins "washed away." The passages are all beautifully harmonious. There is more evidence. We understand that when one becomes saved he begins a new life in Christ. Al now is teaching that this may occur prior to water baptism. Is that what Paul believed and taught?

What did Paul believe and teach?

In Romans 6:3,4 Paul compared the new life of Christ at his resurrection *to our new life as we are raised from baptism.* To argue that our new life in Christ began *before* baptism is like arguing that Jesus' new life began *before* his resurrection. Some of

Al's arguments reflect a rather strange way of reasoning. He delights in using the illustration of one's nose breaking the surface of water in baptism. He challenges people to state the *exact instant* at which the person becomes saved. From the fact that one cannot state authoritatively the exact moment when one becomes saved, Al triumphantly declares that therefore baptism is *not* the point at which one is saved.

Very faulty reasoning! Consider the following: in II Kings 5 we find the story of a leper named Naaman who was told to dip himself seven times in the Jordan River, after which he would be healed. Here is a question for Al: at what *exact moment* was Naaman healed? Was it when his nose broke the surface of the water after the seventh dip? Was it when his entire body emerged? If you do not know the exact moment of the healing, *does that mean that he was not healed at all through the dipping?* In both cases the answer is the same: who knows–*and who cares?* If God says to do something it is foolish for us to try to pin him down to the exact instant when He considers the transaction completed. Why would anyone want to engage in such nonsense? This may make good debating. It fails to make good sense.

When Was Cornelius Saved?

One of the more obvious mistakes Al is making here relates to Cornelius. He insists that Cornelius was saved before baptism. His "proof" is that the Holy Spirit was gifted to the household of Cornelius before they were baptized (Acts 10:44-48). But if the angel of God told the truth they were *not* saved by the baptism in the Spirit! Why do I say so? Consider these facts:

(1) According to Acts 11:11-14, the angel told Cornelius that Peter would bring to him a "**message** through which you and all your household will be saved." A message is not an experience. A message is words. An act is not words.

(2) Please note that Luke, writing very carefully we suppose, wrote in verse 4 that Peter explained to them PRECISELY what

 happened. In verse 15 Peter said, "As I *began* to speak the Holy Spirit came on them. . . "

(3) If the Holy Spirit came on the people as Peter *began* to speak, he obviously had not yet delivered his message–*the one **through which** they were to be saved!*

So when did the Holy Spirit fall on these people? Was it after they heard the "message through which" they would be saved? Or was it *before* they heard the message? This leaves us with a choice: we can believe the angel of God who said that the people would be saved through Peter's message, or we can believe our brother who says they were saved *before* the message was given. With all due respect to Al, I have to go with the angel who was sent from God to start the process by which these first Gentiles were added to the body of Christ.

Acts 11 provides an explanation of why the Holy Sprit fell on these people, and it has nothing to do with whether they were saved by the baptism in the Spirit. It was to convince the Jerusalem leaders when they heard of it, just as it had convinced Peter and his companions, that it was God's will to preach the gospel to and baptize in water Gentiles as well as Jews into Christ. The best that those of Al's persuasion can do with this is to try to think up some definition of "saved" other than the obvious one, and some do exactly that.

Are repentant sinners apt to die prior to baptism? Another of Al's arguments echoes challenges used by believers in conversion by faith alone for generations. They discuss a scenario in which a penitent believer is about to be baptized, but he suddenly dies before he gets to the water (there are different variations of the story, but the point is the same). Then comes the indignant accusation that we would consider that person damned to an eternity in a burning hell when he couldn't help himself, and a loving God would *never* do such a thing. Unfortunately, some of our brethren have fallen for this trap and expressed the view that the person *would* be lost.

WRONG ANSWER – and a very foolish one at that. First of all, the Lord has made it clear that He is the only one in charge of making final judgments, and humans have no business dabbling in such matters. Secondly, our God is the ultimate in fairness and justice. He has absolute authority to make any exceptions to His rules that he deems appropriate. He is master of His rules. The rules are not master of the One who made the rules.

But here is the REAL question: Does the fact that God might make exceptions to a rule *give us the right to ignore or invalidate that rule?* ABSOLUTELY NOT! If God declares that it is through baptism that sins are washed away, as he did through the words spoken in the case of Saul of Tarsus [and often elsewhere, reminds Ray], who are we to deny this fact because we can come up with a situation where it did not work out for a person to be baptized? We must stick with God's rules and let him work out the situations that are problematic!

At what point are believing, repentant sinners saved? In e-mail communications with Al he has elaborated to me somewhat on his views. If one does not receive salvation at baptism, when *does* he receive it? I asked about when Saul of Tarsus was saved? Al expressed the belief that one cannot say exactly *when* one is saved. God knows, but the person cannot be sure. As he put it, "I think we too often get bogged down over 'timing,' especially when our God is not bound by such restraints. **God regards us as saved when one's heart is genuinely given over to him in loving faith. I imagine HE is aware of that happening before we are.**"

I find this view rather amazing! Al taunts those who believe baptism is part of the conversion with the challenge to prove the *exact instant* when one's sins are forgiven, and then admits that he does not know himself when that occurs. No one can really say, then, when he became saved, when he became a Christian. Only God knows, and it may have happened before the person realized it! Wow! This view raises some real questions and has some puzzling implications. First, how much "loving faith" must one have to be saved? (Please note that the Bible says *nothing* about the development of "loving faith" being the point at which one becomes saved.) Ordinarily faith develops gradually and, in fact, continues to grow through the years. How can one know when that faith has developed to the point of being "salvation-worthy"? Since only God knows this, one can only *guess* whether or not he has been saved! *How unsettling!*

Consider the scene on Pentecost. When the convicted crowd asked Peter what they should do, (Peter apparently was not familiar with Al's ideas) he said nothing about believing or having faith. (He seems to have concluded that they *did* believe; otherwise they would not have reacted as they did. It seems likely that their faith was much more of a "fearful" faith than a "loving" faith.) **He told them to repent and be baptized in order to receive forgiveness of sins and the Spirit-gift.**

Some 3,000 were baptized that day and added to the church using *exactly* the formula that Jesus through Peter prescribed. Do you suppose that any of them wondered if they had achieved the level of "loving faith" that Al would consider necessary to receive salvation? Do you suppose they all considered themselves to have fulfilled the Lord's requirements and were indeed saved? Could they tell anyone the *exact* day and hour when they were saved (without a discussion of noses and water surface)? Wouldn't they have supposed it was when they had done what Peter said was required of them?

Finally, consider the following: The real issue in all this can be summed up in one question: **Is the baptism commanded by Jesus a part of the process by which a sinner becomes saved and added to God's church or is baptism as Al now teaches something that occurs some time after one has been saved?**

Certainly God knows the answers and surely he would see to it that the Holy Spirit recorded both of these in the scriptures in the right order. So what are the facts? There are *seven* passages which include *both* baptism and salvation (or the equivalent of being saved): Mark 16:15,16, Acts 2:37,38, Acts 22:16, Romans 6:3,4, Colossians 2:12, Galatians 3:27, and I Peter 3:21. Guess how many of the passages have these in the order which Al advocates (salvation, and *then* baptism)? Answer: ZERO. *Every single passage has baptism before salvation!* It never ceases to amaze me that so many people would choose to ignore the scriptural order and substitute another set of ideas!

Marion D. Owens * Lancaster, California

***

A later letter from Ray Downen.

And here's a letter sent in December, 2011 by Ray Downen to AL MAXEY and others concerning his teaching about a baptism by the Holy Spirit and conversion into Christ. He feels apparently that only his enemies disagree with his recently-revealed theories. But neither Marion nor I are enemies of Al Maxey.

Subject: Al Maxey is a beloved brother–in error.

AL MAXEY exclaims, "The more effectively God uses us in our respective ministries, the more determined *our enemies* become in their efforts to silence us at any cost." And I explain: **We** are not your enemies. As also are Marion Owens and Olan Hicks and many others, I am your friend and brother. You do much that is outstandingly good. I admire the good you do and teach. I freely say so. But now you're also emphasizing doctrine that we see could not be true. **As a real friend I am determined to oppose your *error* in any possible way.**

Jesus commanded that MEN should baptize every new convert (Matthew 28:18-20). Al, are you not saying He really meant that the Spirit would do the baptizing? But that is not at all what Jesus said **or ever in any way implied.** I explain the new birth at length in my book, RAISED INTO NEW LIFE, Part 1 <http://missionoutreach.org/Raysed1.html> or it can be purchased from amazon.com. We think we hear you saying believers are saved prior to the new birth of water and spirit which Jesus says is essential for entrance into His Kingdom.

You posit that the Spirit COMES before He is sent by Jesus to those who obey the gospel, as is promised in Acts 2:38 in the Bible. You quote many other Bible teachers who share your idea about a baptism by the Holy Spirit. I read them and weep. For they do NOT "rightly divide" the inspired Word. They ignore Acts 2:38 as you now apparently are willing also to do. I see no way your brothers and friends can silence your present false teaching except by convincing you to return to teaching only Bible truth. So I'll continue praising the good you do even while I speak as loudly as possible in opposition to the false doctrine now mixed in with the good. I'll share this word with as many who might consider it as I possibly can.– Ray Downen.

***

And Ray further remarks:

My friend & brother Al Maxey has kindly responded to notes I've sent out in which I describe what I hear him now teaching about a second baptism he thinks occurs in every Christian's experience. He affirms that my understanding is not accurate, that my description of what he is teaching is misrepresenting him. He doesn't want to call the baptizing a baptism. He avoids the use of that verb for what he feels Paul says is done by the Holy Spirit to bring a sinner into the body.

Note that **what the apostle wrote** does not claim a baptizing was done by the Spirit. Paul speaks of the human's spirit which must be changed for salvation through new birth. **And everywhere the verb is used in reference to conversion it's translated as "baptizing."**

That Al is sincerely seeking to teach only truth can't be denied. We want to keep it in mind as we evaluate what he is teaching. On Monday, January 2, 2012 at 10:29 PM, Al Maxey sent an e-mail to protest what Marion and I are saying, and to explain that he is not teaching a "baptizing" by the Spirit since he has renamed what the translators refer to as baptizing. He calls it a "plunging" when the apostle's word is universally translated as "baptizing." {RAY: Peter says, "Repent <u>and</u> *be baptized...*"}

I surely do not want to misrepresent Al Maxey–or anyone, even in the slightest. But I read what I read, and I do understand language. And I clearly hear my friend saying that it's the Spirit who baptizes sinners, just as his book title (Immersed by One Spirit) affirms and as he has affirmed on his web site publicly since June 2008. And this is absolutely and entirely foreign to apostolic teaching as I read the New Testament. **Please attend to what Al later wrote in explanation of his teaching:**

> Ray, I have tried and tried and tried to get you to see that I am NOT teaching a Holy Spirit baptism (at least NOT in the sense that you SAY I am). However, I can't seem to get through to you on that, Ray. Anyway, to answer the questions asked by you and Marion: Yes, I believe Peter was speaking of water baptism in Acts 2:38 (I think I made that clear in today's latest issue of Reflections). (Quoted here earlier). Yes, the 3,000 baptized, in my opinion, knew he meant water baptism. I have never denied water baptism *as an essential act of faith.* I state it over and over and over .... etc.
>
> Let me try one more time, Ray–the Greek word "baptizo" has a wide range of meaning, and it is often used by the Greeks to refer to more than just a religious rite of immersion in water. In 1 Corinthians 12:13 the ONLY thing I am trying to get across, Ray, is that when the saved are added to the Lord, and numbered together with the One Body, **it is the Spirit who is said to accomplish this.**
>
> He "plunges" (I'm sorry, Ray, but this is the word Paul used) us into an intimate relationship with our Lord, and, by extension, with one another. I am not preaching some ritualistic Holy Spirit "baptism." *I am just using the word Paul used to indicate that our uniting with the Lord and His people is accomplished by the Spirit, not by any act of any man or religious council.* This teaching in no way removes water baptism, nor repentance, nor faith, etc., as essential re-

sponses of man. Paul is just telling us that it is not MAN who "inserts" us into relationship with the Lord and His people, it is the SPIRIT.

I don't know why you can't grasp this, brother. Instead, you continue to misrepresent my teaching . . . and most likely you will continue to do so. For some strange reason you seem unable to grasp the concept I have stated above (and which Paul also stated to the Corinthian brethren). Have a great evening, Ray, and a very Happy New Year. I hope to see you in Tulsa. – AL.

***

RAY: The Greek original phrase in question, in 1 Corinthians 12:13 simply calls for us to be lovingly united because *we all* (every born-again sinner) *accepted baptism in the same spirit of humble repentance.* I'm sure it's Jesus who adds us to His book of life and brings us into His family, His church, and gives us His Spirit when we have obeyed the gospel. To read it for the meaning **the apostle put there** removes any thought of needing to redefine baptizing as if here the word was being used in a totally different meaning from its obvious meaning in the many other places where the word is used. The phrase is "in one spirit we were all baptized." God's Spirit-gift is clearly mentioned *later* in the verse–all new Christians are made to "drink of" the Spirit.

The word Paul wrote and Al wants to say means "plunges" is everywhere else in apostolic writing transliterated as "baptizes." *It's not clear to me why Al wants to think Paul had a different meaning here than everywhere else.* Nor do I have any reason to believe Jesus can't write our names in His book of Life without help from the Spirit. Jesus commands that PEOPLE are to perform the baptisms which save and bring sinners into the body of Christ. Would Paul have disputed with Jesus as to who performs baptism into the body? Why would anyone think so? Knowing that there is ONE baptism in the Christian way, would Paul have here spoken of a second? And I repeat that the word used by Paul here is everywhere transliterated into English as "baptizes" rather than "plunges." We should understand that Paul was not speaking of anything done by the Holy Spirit in this phrase in 1 Corinthians 12:13 in connection with being brought into the church through baptism. The gift of the Spirit is given to help those now IN Christ Jesus to live for Jesus!

Do apostles call being baptized an “act of faith” *Christians* should perform? Indeed they do not. It’s the unsaved who are to repent and be baptized. The command is NOT to the convert to somehow baptize himself/herself. That might make it an act of faithful obedience. It’s we who tell others about Jesus who are commanded to baptize them. So what’s this about baptism being “an act of faith” on the part of the one accepting baptism rather than simply an act essential for being saved?

As in Acts 2:38, the Spirit of God is given to each sinner who humbly obeys the gospel by repenting and accepting water baptism. But still it’s by order of JESUS that **people** do the baptizing. He didn’t commission the Spirit to do any plunging or dipping as sinners turn to Jesus seeking salvation. Jesus gifts us with His Spirit as we are being reborn. New birth of water and spirit is marvelous. It’s glorious. Remission of sins and the gift of the Spirit come to each person who obeys the gospel of Jesus Christ.

***

A Notable Note by Marion Owens

Al, I must say that I am struck by how complicated your explanations are when compared to simple straight-forward scriptures. I never thought you taught the Holy Spirit baptism argument, nor do I doubt that the Holy Spirit has a role in the conversion process. *He helps **us** as we tell others about JESUS.*

I do believe that you go far beyond the scriptures when you insist that the moment of salvation precedes water baptism. I find it very ironic that you taunt those of us who believe that it is at baptism that one becomes saved (receives forgiveness of sins/has sins washed away, etc.) with the “nose breaking the water surface” argument, but then you concede that you yourself do not know when one becomes saved! I have never before heard of any of our brothers arguing that it is not possible to know when one becomes saved. If you don't know when, you also don't know whether! I find this to be a very disconcerting concept.

I have continued to try to really get a clearer understanding of what you believe, asking specific questions to help me get a practical application of your teachings. That is why I asked if you thought **(1)** the 3,000 on Pentecost were saved before their baptism. And **(2)** how would they know to add 3,000 to their number on Pentecost if no one knew whether or not they were saved? Some time back I asked you **(3)** the precise moment when Naaman's leprosy was healed, and was it at the precise moment when his nose broke the surface of the water?

I was and am disappointed that you did not provide answers to these three questions. To that I would add these questions:

(4) When were Saul's sins "washed away"? Was it at the precise moment when his nose broke the surface of the water? **(5)** Does the fact that you do not know exactly when mean that it did not happen at all? Is it not sufficient that God knows? **(6)** Jesus commands that the convert is to be baptized. Does Jesus know when the act is complete? **(7)** The conversion process is compared to the birth process. Do you ask when the precise instant of physical birth occurs? Is it when the first bodily part emerges? Is it when every last body part is clear? [Ray adds: *Is it when the first breath is taken? That might compare best with the moment when God's "breath," His Spirit, is given to the new Christian–at baptism in water, says Peter*]. **(8)** Does an inability to define the "exact instant" of birth mean that the birth did not occur?

I find your reasoning to be so strange! You seem to echo the faith-alone tenet ruling out baptism as the point of receiving salvation on the basis that baptism is a "work," and since one is not saved "by works," baptism could not be a part of the conversion process. Faith-alone teachers had to address the problem of just WHEN a person becomes saved. Their solution is to have one pray for salvation–the so-called "sinner's prayer." (*This is despite the fact that the Bible says absolutely nothing about anyone ever being told to pray for salvation or anyone ever being saved through prayer.*) A further irony in the conversion by faith-alone teaching is that they say that **one must pray,** which surely involves more "work" than submitting passively while another baptizes him or her!

Some Pentecostals and others go a bit farther than some others who teach conversion by faith alone. They commonly have people come to a "mourner's bench" and engage in extended, often agonizing, pleading with God to save them as if God is really reluctant to provide salvation and needs an awful lot of prodding!! [RAY: *Does the Word still say "**Whosoever will** may come*"? (John 3:16,36 and Revelation 22:17)]

Several of your statements seem to imply that a man can do nothing to help facilitate his salvation, and that to do so would somehow violate the principle of salvation by grace through faith. Surely you are aware of God's long history of rewarding a *demonstrated* faith. This has nothing to do with any sort of "salvation by works." It has happened over and over. The lepers were to go show themselves to the priest. The blind man was to wash in the pool of Siloam. Naaman was to dip in the Jordan River. Abraham was to sacrifice his son. And on and on. In none of these cases were the blessings the result of their own efforts. It was always through **God's power reacting to demonstrations of faith.** Is it not precisely the same with baptism?

No one claims that anything in water itself washes away sins (any more than anything in the Jordan cured Naaman's leprosy). Those who pretend that we believe that baptismal water heals or in itself by itself washes away sin are both cynical and dishonest. Finally, as I read the scriptures and see the messages and instructions given to the first converts to Christianity, I can only imagine how bewildered and perplexed they would have been had they tried to figure out the complex set of principles which you have come to embrace. (I have been around for nearly eighty years and I am having a heck of a time trying to figure out what you are saying!). Thanks, Marion.

***

Wrap-Up Writings by Ray

I can understand and appreciate what Al writes all right. But his teaching on conversion indeed is complicated and obviously is based on *faulty* reasoning. How do Al's theories about the text of Acts 2:38 compute with the Way being understood by even the very simple? When Peter preached, he was heard and understood by "simple" seekers. Marion rightly points out that what Al wants us to believe about conversion is not simple truth if it were even truth at all. I do not read in the Bible that the Holy Spirit is involved in conversion prior to the time Peter says He is. That's as God's gift AFTER the new birth is complete (Acts 2:38). The babe's first breath is AFTER the baby is born. An apt comparison is with the breath (pneuma=spirit or wind) of God given at a sinner's new birth of water and spirit.

And since Jesus keeps the book of life, I'm thinking that it's Jesus who saves and adds to His church. Interested readers also might notice an article about the influence of ROBERT RICHARDSON <http://missionoutreach.org/cu-b07.pdf> as written by A. J. Albert in his November 2011 California letter.

And do read my comments about a similar heresy taught by Jack Cottrell, long-time professor at Cincinnati Bible Seminary at <http://missionoutreach.org/tyranny.html>. It includes: *Jack Cottrell points out well that faith alone is dead just as James earlier reported. But it seems to me that he and others miss the mark in claiming that a second baptism, by the Spirit, is always done somehow as proclaimers of the gospel baptize converts in water.*

Any baptism performed by the Spirit would obviously not be a baptism in water. Baptism by the Spirit (if it exists) and baptism as Jesus commanded it to be performed are two separated actions. One is performed by humans. The other is not. They are separate actions if indeed there is in fact a baptism performed by the Holy Spirit. I see no reason to accept this theory as apostolic teaching. Al Maxey, who is right on so many question, has this idea which I think is non-apostolic and obviously incorrect. I refer readers to his study quoted earlier here and at: <http://www.zianet.com/maxey/reflx353.htm>.

Where is there in our Bibles any mention of a baptism by the Holy Spirit except in a mistranslation of 1 Corinthians 12:13? The baptism Paul speaks of in that verse is one which all Christians have experienced, and that Paul knew they knew they had experienced. Paul would no more have claimed that everyone's immersion was performed by the Holy Spirit than he would have denied that Jesus appeared to him on the road to Damascus. What could the apostle hope to gain by introducing something totally unknown when his aim was to UNITE all who knew they had been immersed in water as Jesus commanded? And those to whom he wrote all knew it was human hands which had lowered them and raised them up into the new life!

Some translators use a phrase often properly and correctly translated as "in one spirit" (note NO capitalization) and turn it into "BY the one Spirit." Is there any other mention of a baptism by the Spirit in inspired writings? No. Not one. The baptism commanded by Jesus is performed by proclaimers of the gospel. It's in water. Christian baptism is a *burial of a sinner,* and a RESURRECTION INTO NEW LIFE, raised OUT OF a watery tomb (see Romans 6). The Spirit is promised as a gift to those believers in Jesus who repent and ARE baptized in water in recognition of the Lordship of Jesus of Nazareth. The inspired writers said nothing of a baptism by the Holy Spirit. Not once. Never.

Instead, Jesus commands that we who tell others about Him are to baptize those who believe! WE are to perform the "one baptism" Paul speaks of in Ephesians 4:5, in 1 Corinthians 12:13, and in many other apostolic writings. As promised, God's Spirit is gifted to each believer who repents and in water is baptized into Christ (Acts 2:38). Salvation in Christ prior to and separate from the baptism commanded by Jesus is not Christian doctrine any way you read it.

***

A later Word from Al Maxey

July 1, 2012 via e-mail:

Good Afternoon Ray, I guess one of my biggest frustrations right now is that I cannot seem to get you to grasp that I am NOT teaching a 2nd baptism. {RAY: The Greek manuscripts and translators think it's baptism, but Al says it isn't.}

And I am certainly not teaching a "baptism" that replaces or negates a believer's immersion in water. ALL I have sought to convey is that what Paul is teaching us in the 1 Corinthians 12:13 passage is that the One who places us within our relationship with the Lord Jesus Christ is the Spirit. {RAY: Paul wrote "in one spirit we all were **baptized** INTO the one body."}

The word Paul used in that passage to convey this idea of "placing within" is the Greek word "baptizo" (frankly, I wish sometimes that he had picked a different word, as it seems to be the word itself over which you are stumbling here). {RAY: I'm stumbling and didn't even know it!?}

He did not use that word of any kind of religious ritual in water, but merely sought to convey that our union with the Lord is accomplished by the Spirit. {RAY: Jesus used the word in His commission to the apostles. He commanded that they were to carry the gospel everywhere they went and THEY were to BAPTIZE those who believed. Was He speaking of some kind of "religious ritual" or something the Holy Spirit was going to do?}

That in no way removes our obligation to respond in faith to His gift of grace by being immersed in water. The latter is a very special rite, and one that we must preach and practice. In Scripture we know that we who are saved are "added to the Lord" and also numbered together with all others who are thus added to Him. Paul simply informs us that it is the Spirit who adds us to

Him. Thus, it is truly a union/unity of the Spirit, and not of man. {RAY: But what the apostle says is that in one spirit we were all **baptized** into the body which we call the church. And every one of those baptisms was performed by human hands as Jesus commanded.}

To say that the Spirit is the One who unites us with the Lord, who places us in relationship with Him (who "plunges" us into that saving relationship) is NOT teaching a "second baptism." Ray, WHY can't you see that?!!!! {RAY: Because the verb used by Paul is the same verb used by Jesus when He commanded that people who now believed should be baptized! So I see no good reason to give the word here a different meaning than all the translators do.}

I fear you can't get past the use of the term "baptizo" in 1 Corinthians 12:13, and can ONLY see it as "water" baptism (although this is a term used variously by the Greeks). {RAY: My brother, I have never seen any translation from the Greek which put any word in the apostle's mouth (hand) in this verse except baptized. Are there accepted translations which change from that translation?}

I simply suggest, as have other biblical scholars, that Paul used that word to show the action of the Spirit in effecting this union with the Lord of a penitent believer ... a believer who, by the way, evidences that marvelous saving union by an act of faith in which he is immersed in water. Again, it frustrates me to no end that I can't get this distinction through to you. Perhaps the fault lies with me; maybe I'm just not able to explain it adequately for you to grasp it (although most other people I talk to say that it is very easy to understand, and they too wonder why you can't grasp it). Anyway, I love you, brother. Have a super week. – AL.

{RAY: I love and respect Al Maxey. I'm sorry indeed that he is now teaching a second baptism for entrance into Christ's body, this one performed by the Holy Spirit. Since he is wrong in this I see no way to agree with him.}

***

J. James Albert speaks to the question "Is God more strict and stringent when it comes to 'the worship assembly' than He is for our daily living?" He writes, My unelaborated answer is I don't think so, but let me elaborate.

First of all I see the idea that God is more demanding and strict when it comes to the alleged worship assembly growing out of the legalistic philosophy that the new covenant scriptures are a code of law and we are saved by our rightness, either wholly or partially. Second, it is a defense of unwritten creeds which most often pertain to the so-called "five acts of worship" and the unscriptural practices of fellowship associated with these creeds. Third, this idea reflects a misunderstanding of worship, not only implying precepts that are not biblical in regard to the assembling of believers, but is indicative of being a spin-off of the devilish sacred-secular approach to life.

Even under the Law of Moses God did not consider worship which involved required burnt offerings and sacrifices more important than aspects of daily living. Solomon said, "To do righteousness and justice is more acceptable to the Lord than sacrifice" (Proverbs 21:3). Then Hosea 6:6 says, "For I desire mercy and not sacrifice, and the knowledge of God more than burnt offerings." Jesus quoted Hosea 6:6 at least twice during his earthly ministry (Matthew 9:13; 12:7).

Does the Sermon On The Mount indicate that God puts more emphasis upon the acts or rituals of our assembling than He does our lifestyle? This is Jesus' most elaborate teaching in the new covenant scriptures, and the emphasis is upon lifestyle, ethical and moral and righteous living, not "acts of worship" when we assemble. In Matthew 5:22-24 he says that brotherly relationships are more important than formal worship.

What did Jesus say were the two greatest commandments? "Assemble correctly and exclude those who do not agree." Of course I jest. Just after he answered the lawyer's question Jesus scathingly rebuked the scribes and Pharisees for many of the practices related to the worship of the Temple while neglecting "the weightier matters of the law: justice and mercy and faith."

The fact is that the new covenant scriptures say very little about what we are to do when we assemble, and many of our "laws" and methods("acts") are based upon the silence of the scriptures, using implications and inferences. The primary purpose of assembling is for believers to edify one another, as Hebrews 10:25 states. Even Paul's concern when he wrote the most about assembling we have in the scriptures was the behavior of believers in regard to one another, relationships, not the mechanics or methodology.

Over the years a cardinal rule of Bible interpretation has been that what is the most clear is the most important. What is the most clear in the new covenant writings has to do with ethical and moral living. Even the most specific case of actual excluding from fellowship has to do with moral turpitude (1 Corinthians 5). Nowhere in the scriptures are we commanded to exclude from our fellowship brethren who merely disagree with us regarding "matters of faith" per se relative to "acts" of the assembly, as we have done and do. Brethren often try to make a case that those who disagree are divisive on that basis, but that is not true. Those who proceed to blackball and exclude and "disfellowship," as we say, on that premise are the contentious and divisive ones.

One more citation. What did James say was "Pure and undefiled religion before God and the Father"? "To be correct and right in the five 'acts of worship' in our assembling." Again, I jest. He said, "to visit orphans and widows in their trouble, and to keep oneself unspotted from the world." To be of service to others and live holy lives! If the most important aspect of being a Christian was the "acts" of our assembling, and therein was where God was going to judge us the most strict, why didn't James so specify?

So there you have my elaboration. Let me close with something brother Leroy Garrett wrote in What Must the Church of Christ Do To Be Saved? "The most serious error is to be proud, arrogant, and judgmental. These are the sins our Lord condemned. Some people are sincerely mistaken about things we suppose to be right. That doesn't keep them from being Christians, unless we presume that a Christian has to render perfect obedience and have perfect knowledge."

***

I invite your attention to other studies on becoming a Christian. One title is "Three Times Peter used the KEYS of the Kingdom" (Viewpoint HS-J01). An interesting study is "About Entering Christ's Way" (Viewpoint FA-C02). "Were You BUR-

 IED With Christ?" by Gaylon Embrey is CB-H01. Available from amazon.com is RAISED INTO NEW LIFE, Part 1 which deals extensively with the new birth of water and spirit. I can mail you 5 copies for a gift of $20.00 (including postage).

Another title is "RAISED INTO NEW LIFE with Christ" by Ray Downen (Viewpoint PB-Z01 206 pages, available from amazon.com). And CD-F01, by Boyce Mouton, is "We Are Invited to Enter Into COVENANT With God." "PROPER Bible Understanding" is PB-P01, with "Rules for Right Reading" being PB-I01.

Others can join me in speaking out for truth and for unity in Jesus. My doing so is as Mission Outreach Publications, with mailing address at P O Box 265, Joplin MO 64802-0265. For a gift of $25 I can mail you 5 copies of this booklet you could then share with others. As well as sharing publications with others, you can help by sharing in expenses of the mission. Gifts are not tax deductible but will go toward publishing and promoting written material such as the booklet you have in your hands or are reading otherwise. Gifts are needed.

– Ray Downen, Mission Outreach Publications, Inc.

MISSION OUTREACH * OWENS-MAXEY-DOWNEN * CD-K01 * 12/29/2012

www.ingramcontent.com/pod-product-compliance
Lightning Source LLC
LaVergne TN
LVHW010546100826
845148LV00013B/2623

* 9 7 8 1 6 0 6 5 8 0 2 4 0 *